EXPLORING THE COUNTRIES IN THE GROUP OF EIGHT

Geography for Grade 6

Children's Geography & Culture Books

BABY PROFESSOR

EDUCATION KIDS

Speedy Publishing LLC

40 E. Main St. #1156

Newark, DE 19711

www.speedypublishing.com

Copyright 2017

The Group of Eight, also referred to as G8, is a group of leaders around the world that meet to discuss global issues on an annual basis. In this book, we will be learning more about the member countries of the Group of Eight.

G8 MEMBERS

The Group of Eight consists of the heads of government from France, Germany, Italy, Japan, Russia, Canada, the United States, and the United Kingdom. The European Union is represented as well at the summits by the European Commission president as well as the leader of the country having the European Union presidency.

UNITED KINGDOM

GERMANY

ITALY

CANADA

RUSSIA

USA

FRANCE

JAPAN

The 1976 original members of the G8 included Germany, France, Japan, Italy, the United States and

the United Kingdom, and were joined later in 1976 by Canada, and in 1998 Russia was added.

GERMANY

For several centuries, the land that is now considered as Germany was previously inhabited by Germanic speaking tribes. Originally, they would become a part of the Frankish Empire under rule of Charlemagne, who was known as the father of the German Monarchy. Most of Germany would then become a part of the Holy Roman Empire.

World War 1

The Kingdom of Prussia was established in Germany from 1700 to 1918. World War I broke out in 1914 and Germany was part of the side that lost and approximately 2 million soldiers died during the war.

Germany attempted to recover in the wake of the war. The monarchy collapsed after there was a revolution and it wasn't too long after that when Adolf Hitler rose to power. Hitler started the Nazi party, which believed the German race to be superior. He became dictator and proceeded to expand the German empire.

The Reichstag building

He started World War II and would conquer most of Europe, including France. The United States, Britain, and the Allies, however, managed to defeat him. Germany was then divided into two separate countries, West Germany and East Germany.

East Germany became a communist state that was under Soviet Union control, and West Germany was free. The Berlin Wall was constructed between East Germany and West Germany to keep people from fleeing from the East to the West. In 1989, the wall was torn down. West Germany and East Germany became one country on October 3, 1990.

The remains of the Berlin Wall

Eiffel Tower, Paris

FRANCE

France, which is officially known as the French Republic, is a country that consists of territory in the western section of Europe as well as many overseas territories and regions. The European (metropolitan) area stretches from the English Channel to the Mediterranean Sea and to the North Sea, and from the Rhine river to the Atlantic Ocean. It also includes French Guiana located on the continent of South America as well as many islands in the Indian, Pacific, and Atlantic oceans.

France's 18 integral regions, of which 5 are located overseas, span a total area of 643,801 sq. km. which equals 248,573 sq. miles. The total population as of January 2017 is approximately 67 million people. France is considered a unitary semi-presidential republic and its capital is Paris, which is its largest city and leading commercial and cultural center. Other major urban cities include Lyon, Marseille, Lille, Toulouse, Bordeaux, and Nice.

Paris, France

Mt. Fuji, Japan

JAPAN

Japan is a sovereign island nation that is located in East Asia. It is located in the Pacific, lies off the east coast of the mainland of Asia, and stretches from the the East China Sea towards the southwest and the Sea of Okhotsk towards the north.

Consisting of approximately 6,852 islands, Japan is known as a stratovolcanic archipelago. The largest four islands are Shikoku, Kyushu, Hokkaido, and Honshu, making up around 97% of its land area and are often referred to as the home islands. Japan is divided into 47 prefectures in 8 regions; with Hokkaido being the northernmost, and Okinawa being the southernmost. Its population of approximately 127 million makes it the eleventh largest country in the world. Japan's total population is comprised of about 98.5% Japanese. About 9.1 million people live in the capital of Japan, which is Tokyo.

Japan

Grand Canal, Italy

ITALY

Italy, which is officially known as the Italian Republic, is considered a parliamentary, unitary republic located in Europe, in the heart of the Mediterranean Sea. It shares open land borders with Vatican City, San Marino, Slovenia, Austria, Switzerland and France. It covers an area of 301,338 km2, which equals 116,347 sq. miles, and experiences a temperate seasonal Mediterranean climate. It is often referred to as the Boot (lo Stivale) because of its shape. Italy is the fourth highest populous EU member state, having 61 million inhabitants.

Italy currently has the Eurozone's third greatest GDP (Gross Domestic Product) and is eighth in the world. Its advanced economy makes it sixth in national wealth throughout the world. Italy has an extremely high level of human development, ranking sixth for life expectancy around the world. It plays a key role in global and regional cultural, military, diplomatic, and economic affairs, and it is considered a regional power as well as a great power. It is a founding member and leading member of the European Union and is a member of many international institutions, including, but not limited to, the UN, NATO, the G7/G8, and the G20. As reflected in its cultural wealth, it is home to 51 World Heritage Sites (the most throughout the world) and is the world's fifth most visited country.

Pisa Cathedral

River Thames, England, United Kingdom

UNITED KINGDOM

Commonly referred to as the United Kingdom, UK, or Britain, the United Kingdom of Great Britain and Northern Ireland, which can be found in western Europe, is a sovereign country. Located off of the north-west coast of the mainland of Europe, the UK consists of the north-east section of the island of Ireland, the island of Great Britain, as well as several smaller islands.

English Channel

The only section of the UK sharing a land border with a second sovereign state is Northern Ireland, sharing the border with the Republic of Ireland. Other than this land border, it is bordered by the Atlantic, the English Channel to the south, the North Sea to the east, and the Celtic Sea to the south-south-west, which gives it the world's 12th-longest coastline. The Irish Sea is located between Ireland and Great Britain.

Tower Bridge, London, United Kingdom

The UK is the 8th-largest sovereign state in the world and Europe's 11th-largest, having an area of 242,500 sq. km. (93,600 sq. miles). With approximately 65.1 million inhabitants, it is considered to be the 21st-most populous country.

The UK is a constitutional monarchy along with a parliamentary democracy. Queen Elizabeth II is the monarch and has held this title since February 6, 1952. Its largest city and capital is London, which is a financial center and global city having an urban area population of 10.3 million, which makes it the second-largest in the European Union and fourth-largest of Europe. Its other major urban areas include Leeds, Liverpool, Glasgow, and Manchester. The UK is comprised of four countries; Northern Ireland, Wales, Scotland, and England.

Aerial view of the Thames and London City

UNITED STATES

The United States of America, also referred to as the United States, the U.S., and USA, is a federal republic that is comprised of 50 states, a federal district, five self-governing territories, as well as various possessions. Of the 50 states, 48 are contiguous, as well as the federal district, and are located in North America between Mexico and Canada.

Alaska is located at the northwest corner of North America, bordered towards the east by Canada and from Russia towards the west, across the Bering Strait. Hawaii is located in the middle of the Pacific Ocean and is an archipelago. The territories of the United States are scattered throughout the Caribbean Sea and the Pacific Ocean, across nine various time zones. The extremely diverse wildlife, climate, and geography of the United States makes it one of the top 17 megadiverse countries throughout the world.

Bering Strait

The U.S. is the third-largest or fourth-largest country throughout the world by total area, the third-largest throughout the world by land area, and the third-most populated country through the world. It is known as one of the most multicultural and ethnically diverse nations around the world and is home to the largest population of immigrants throughout the world.

Washington, D.C. is the capital of the United States. New York City is the largest city, and nine other major cities, have at least 4.5 million inhabitants – San Francisco, Boston, Atlanta, Miami, Philadelphia, Houston, Dallas, Chicago, and Los Angeles.

Washington DC

False Creek and the Burrard Street Bridge in Vancouver, Canada

CANADA

Canada is located at the northern area of North America. It consists of three territories and ten provinces and extends from the Pacific Ocean to the Atlantic Ocean and northward towards the Arctic Ocean, which covers a total of 9.98 million sq. km. (3.85 million sq. miles). Its sole border along the United States is the longest bi-national land border throughout the world. Most of the country's climate is either cold or brutally cold during the winter, although areas to the south are warmer in the summer.

Canada's population is sparse, with most of its land territory dominated by tundra and forest as well as the Rocky Mountains. With 82% of its 35.15 million people found in medium and larger-sized cities, it is highly urbanized, with many located near the border to the south. Ottawa is the capital of Canada, and Vancouver, Montreal, and Toronto are its biggest metropolitan areas.

Flatiron Building, Toronto Cannada

Canada is a constitutional monarchy and federal parliamentary democracy, and Queen Elizabeth II is the head of state. It is officially a bilingual country at the federal level. Canada is known to be one of the most multicultural and ethnically diverse nations throughout the world, which has resulted from the large-scale immigration from several other countries. Relying mainly on is well-developed international trade networks and abundant natural resources, its advanced economy has become the tenth-largest in the world. Its complex and long-standing relationship with the United States has had a tremendous impact on its culture and economy.

RUSSIA

Russia, which is officially referred to as the Russian Federation is a country located in Eurasia. It is the largest country around the world by surface area, at 17, 075,200 sq. km., and covers over one-eighth of Earth's land area that is considered inhabited. With more than 144 million people (March 2016), it is the ninth most populous country.

Saint Petersburg, Russia

Moscow City

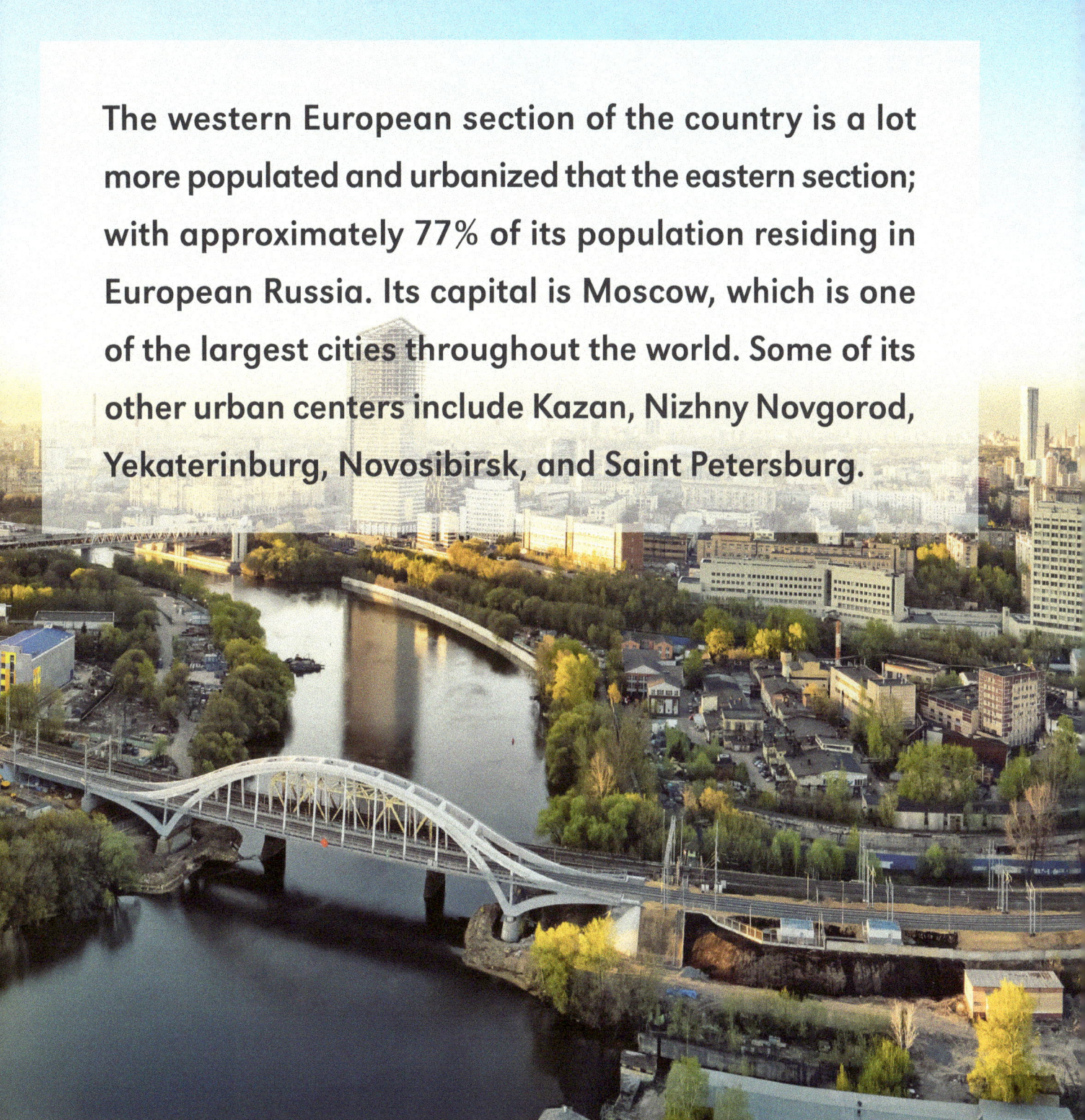

The western European section of the country is a lot more populated and urbanized that the eastern section; with approximately 77% of its population residing in European Russia. Its capital is Moscow, which is one of the largest cities throughout the world. Some of its other urban centers include Kazan, Nizhny Novgorod, Yekaterinburg, Novosibirsk, and Saint Petersburg.

Russia extends entirely across Northern Asia as well as much of Eastern Europe, spanning 11 time zones and incorporates a large range of landforms and environments. From the southeast to the northwest, it shares land borders with North Korea, Mongolia, China, Kazakhstan, Azerbaijan, Georgia, Ukraine, Belarus, Poland (both with Oblast and Kaliningrad), Lithuania, Latvia, Estonia, Finland, and Norway. Russia shares maritime borders with the state of Alaska (United States) across the Bering Strait as well as Japan by the Sea of Okhotsk.

Khabarovsk region, Far East, Russia

G20

The Group of Twenty

Even though we now have the Group of 20, the G8 continues to play an important role in global issues and the economy throughout the world.

For additional information about the G8, you can visit your local library, research the internet, and ask questions of your teachers, family, and friends.

Visit

BABY PROFESSOR
EDUCATION KIDS

www.BabyProfessorBooks.com

to download Free Baby Professor eBooks
and view our catalog of new and exciting
Children's Books

Milton Keynes UK
Ingram Content Group UK Ltd.
UKHW050830060924
447802UK00003BA/103